Know About
Dr. Jagadish Chandra Bose

MAPLE KIDS

Published by

MAPLE PRESS PRIVATE LIMITED
office: A-63, Sector 58, Noida 201301, U.P., India
phone: +91 120 455 3581, 455 3583
email: info@maplepress.co.in
website: www.maplepress.co.in

Reprinted in 2019

ISBN: 978-93-50334-24-9

Contents

Preface

Dr. Jagadish Chandra Bose was a great biologist who proved that plants too can feel in their own way. He saved money, bought a small laboratory and built his equipments. Scientists in Europe and America wondered at his discoveries. He was a true patriot and a great man.

Suppose there is a lush green plant and its leaves are sparkling green in the shining sunlight. You feel like pulling out a leaf to feel it. But, you do not think of what goes on inside the plant. May be, you feel that the plant does not suffer like you, but it does. In fact, the pulsation of the plant stops at the spot where the leaf was plucked. In a short while, the pulsation again begins at the spot, but this time it is very slow. And then it completely stops. That spot is dead for the plant.

It was Jagadish Chandra Bose, an eminent Indian Scientist, who explained that plants also suffer pain like human beings. Though he worked in other fields of Science, he is best known for his research into the life of plants. This book sums up his life events with the achievements he made.

CHAPTER 1
Birth

Jagadish Chandra Bose was born on November 30, 1858, in Faridpur, in Dacca district. Until 1947, Faridpur was a part of India, but now it is in Bangladesh. His mother was a charming lady and was very affectionate towards him. His father, Bhagawan Chandra Bose, was the Deputy Magistrate of Faridpur. He possessed excellent qualities and helped the needy and poor people a lot. He was very compassionate towards the people in sorrow. In the year 1880, a famine hit Bengal. Bhagawan Chandra Bose spent a lot in the rescue work. Once, when the poor villagers suffered due to malaria, Bhagawan Chandra Bose helped the poor families. There were thousands of children, who lost their parents, so he helped those orphans. He also spent his own money and started a factory, so as to provide a means of survival for those orphans. He never regretted helping people from his own pocket.

During those days, the people who were well educated and well off were attracted by the impact of Western culture. People used to feel great if they knew English.

Jagadish Chandra Bose received a remarkable education. This was all because of his father. About a hundred years ago, Bhagawan Chandra Bose started schools, in which children were taught in Bengali. Jagadish was very friendly with poor boys and played with them. This was how he got to know the sufferings of the poor people. He came to know about many more things. He learnt how the fisher folk moved on the broad rivers in their boats, how the fishing rod was cast into the flowing water, how ploughing the land and sowing seeds in it grew the crops and how the cattle were taken to graze on the distant hills. He used to listen to the fishermen and the farmers very carefully, when they gave such accounts. He loved such adventurous life and, thus, became very courageous.

He was having another interesting character in his early life. This was a servant who used to go with Jagadish Chandra to school every day. He was a dacoit earlier and Jagadish's father, as a judge, had sent him to jail. After the punishment period got over, he was released from the jail. But, now he faced the difficulty of making his living. As you have already read that Bhagawan Chandra Bose was very compassionate at heart, so he employed him as his servant. The servant used to tell Jagadish about his robbery stories and his evil deeds. Jagadish liked to listen to his adventures a lot.

CHAPTER 2
Bose - A Curious Kid

Young Bose was all full of curiosity. He wanted to know about everything that happened around him. What is a glow-warm? Is it fire or spark? Why does the wind blow? Why does the water flow? He was always ready with a string of questions. His father would answer as many questions as he could. But he never tried to impress upon his son that he knew everything. If he could not answer a question, he would frankly tell his son so. Thus, Jagadish Chandra's parents took great interest not only in his studies, but also in everything that shaped his character. They narrated stories from the Ramayana and the Mahabharata to him. Karna of Mahabharata was an ideal to him. (Karna was a great hero who was very generous.)

Bose would often go with his parents to watch the performances of folk drama (these were staged in open-air theatres). His parents treated all his friends alike. Such was the environment of Jagadish Chandra's house in his childhood. He grew up to be broad-minded, patriotic boy who was obedient to elders and affectionate towards his fellowmen. He never made any distinction between the rich and the poor, all men were equal in his eyes. Hence, he had all the ingredients of a good human being.

Generally, it is easy to understand a subject if it is taught in the student's language. The subject becomes difficult if it is taught in some other language. Since Jagadish studied the subjects in his own language, he did not face this problem. He understood them easily. He was in the habit of thinking for himself whenever he studied. He learnt many things on his own by studying at home. But, he was not a bookworm and was very enthusiastic about games too. Cricket was his favourite sport.

At the age of nine, a new chapter began in Jagadish Chandra Bose's life. He had to leave his hometown. He

went to the big city of Calcutta for further education. He was admitted to Saint Xavier's School. There was a lot of difference between the previous school and the present one.

CHAPTER 3
A Born Scientist

In Faridpur, Bose had studied everything in his own language. But here, in Calcutta, his schoolmates knew only English. The city boys, especially the English boys, teased him. One of them even hurt Jagadish Chandra, in a bout of boxing. Jagadish was provoked and taught the boy a well-deserved lesson. That was the end to all the teasing.

While he was studying at Saint Xavier's, School, Jagadish Chandra was staying at a boarding house. He had no friends and was lonely here.

But, he was a born scientist. Even as a boy, he had many hobbies, which showed his scientific interest. He used to breed frogs and fishes in a nearby pond. He would pull out a germinating plant and observe its root system. He also had a number of pets like rabbits, squirrels and non-poisonous snakes. Even in Calcutta, he continued these hobbies to get over his solitude. He grew flower-bearing plants and had animals and birds as pets. He did well in his studies and was in the forefront. The teachers liked him for his intelligence. Jagadish Chandra passed the school's final examination in the first class.

He joined the B.A. class in the college. In those days, Science subjects formed a part of this course. He was

most interested in Biology (the Science of life), but Father Lafont, a famous professor of physics, inculcated in Bose, a great interest in the Science of physics. Bose became his favourite student. Though Bose was always interested in any branch of Science, Botany, the Science of plants, still attracted him much.

By the age of nineteen, Jagadish Chandra was a Bachelor of Arts. He wanted to go to England for higher studies. He wished to try his luck at the Indian Civil Service Examination, or to study medicine. If he entered the civil service, he would have been a government officer. This would mean sub-ordination, but his father did not want Jagadish to assist others. On the other hand, he did not have enough money to send the boy abroad. Besides, he wanted that his son should become a teacher and serve his people and his country. Even Jagadish Chandra's mother was not quite willing to send him because she thought it as against their religion. She was pained at the thought that her son would be far away from her. Jagadish Chandra Bose did not wish to do anything against the will of his parents.

CHAPTER 4
From Learning to Teaching

After much contemplation, Bose's mother allowed him to go. She had saved some money. She also wanted to sell her jewels to meet the expenses of her son's voyage. Bhagawan Chandra Bose prevented her to do so and managed to find the money on his own.

At last, in the year 1880, Jagadish went on his way to England. Twenty-two-year-old Jagadish Chandra Bose

stepped into the ship and with that he was stepping into a new phase of life, which laid the foundations of a brilliant future.

In London, he first studied medicine. But he repeatedly fell ill. So, he had to discontinue the course. Then, he studied natural science in the Christ Church College, Cambridge. It was necessary to learn Latin in order to study natural science, which Jagadish had already learnt. He passed Die Tripos examination with distinction. In addition to the Cambridge Tripos examination, he passed the Bachelor of Science examination of London University.

When Jagadish Chandra Bose was back in India, he joined the staff of the Presidency College, Calcutta. There was a peculiar practice in that college. The Indian teachers in the college were paid one third of what the British teachers were paid. So, Jagadish Chandra Bose refused his salary, but worked there for three years. He could not even get the scientific instruments he needed for research. This did not continue for long. His deep knowledge, zest for work and cultured behaviour won over those in charge of the college. They saw to it that he was given the full salary of the post and not one-third.

Teaching the same lessons year in and year out was very tedious to Bose. He had an alert mind, always on the look out for new ideas. He wanted to do research to widen his knowledge and discover new things.

A laboratory is necessary for research. Many scientific instruments are required. Jagadish Chandra Bose had no laboratory and instruments. But he was not disheartened. For eight or ten years, he spent as little out of his salary as possible, lived a very strict life, saved money and bought a laboratory.

CHAPTER 5
Rising Fame

Generally Marconi's name is associated with the invention of wireless (this made possible the use of the radio). Jagadish Chandra Bose had also conducted independent research in the same field. Marconi was able to announce the result of his work and showed how wireless telegraphy worked, earlier than Jagadish Chandra Bose. So, he is called 'the father of the radio'. In the year 1896, Bose wrote a

research article on electromagnetic waves. This impressed the Royal Society of England (which is famous all over the world). He was honoured with the degree of 'Doctor of Science'. He needed money to continue his work. Bengal, his homeland, came forward to bear the expenses. Those were the days when the British Government would not help an Indian to go abroad for studies. Bose had the honour of getting encouragement even from the British Government and he made excellent use of this.

Bose became famous in the world of Science. In India and in other countries there was a strong belief that only Westerners could achieve anything worthwhile in Science. Bose proved this as a wrong concept. He showed that there were geniuses elsewhere too. He visited England again, this time to explain his discoveries to the scientists of the West.

Bose needed scientific equipments. But the instruments he needed were not available. But this did not hamper his work. Earlier in his life, he had learnt to make equipments with his own hands. The scientific instruments he took to England were those which he had made himself.

Electricity was then his special field of work. He successfully worked at transmitting electro-magnetic waves from one place to another and determined the type of instruments required both at the transmitting end, and at the receiving end. He also found out the distance between the two ends. He was using the instruments he had made himself. The gathering of scientists at the Royal Society in England, was profoundly impressed with Bose's work. They praised this achievement as a singular one from a citizen of India. Our country was until then

ছাত্রবৃন্দসহ আচার্য জগদীশচন্দ্র বসু
উপবিষ্ট। বাম দিক থেকে : মেঘনাদ সাহা, জগদীশচন্দ্র, জ্ঞানচন্দ্র ঘোষ
দণ্ডায়মান। বাম দিক থেকে : স্নেহময় দত্ত, সত্যেন্দ্রনাথ বসু, দেবেন্দ্রমোহন বসু, নিখিলরঞ্জন সেন, জ্ঞানেন্দ্রনাথ মুখোপাধ্যায়, নগেন্দ্রচন্দ্র না'

famous only as the home of Philosophy and religion. Bose won respect for Indians in Science too. The renowned papers of London namely 'The Spectator' and 'The Times' were all praise for this Indian Scientist. Without proper facilities and with the available material, Bose had achieved wonderful results and he had done his search along with his teaching work.

CHAPTER 6
More Inventions

After he lectured at the Royal Society, scientific associations in many other countries invited Jagadish Chandra Bose. He visited France, Germany, America and Japan besides England. He lectured at several places and explained his discoveries.

When electricity passes through a man, animal or plant, they feel a 'shock'. When it is passed through a living being, the being gets excited or 'irritated'. Bose developed an instrument that would show such a reaction of the organism on a graph. When electricity was passed through zinc, a non-living substance, a similar graph was obtained. So, he came to the conclusion that living and non-living things were very similar in certain reactions.

In Paris, he gave a lecture on this similarity between the living and the non-living world. Have you heard of 'radar'? This is a very wonderful scientific device. Sailors on the sea use it. It is also used to get information about aeroplanes coming towards a place. So, you see how useful it is during a war. If the aeroplanes of the enemy try to attack a city, the radar shows their movement. J.C. Bose worked out some details of very great importance that are being used in the working of the radar. When Jagadish Chandra Bose again visited England, Cambridge University honoured him as a professor.

Generally, when a man invents something new, he declares that nobody can make use of it without his permission. If anybody desires to make use of it, he will have to pay him money. This is because the inventor has worked hard and he spent his time and used brain for his invention. It is not right to make use of his work without paying him. An inventor can make lakhs of rupees by just one or two inventions. Bose had invented many instruments. They have since been used by many industries. However, when Bose was offered money for

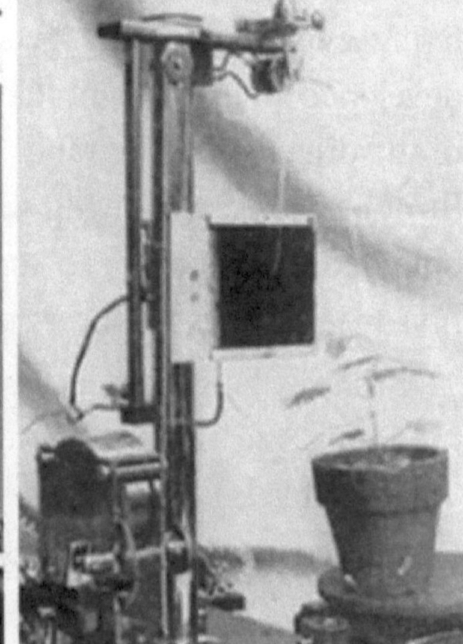

these, he did not accept it. He was very generous and noble. He felt that knowledge was not any one's personal property. He permitted every one the use of the fruits of his work.

The Davy-Faraday Research Institute is a very famous scientific institute for scientific research in England. This institute requested Jagadish Chandra Bose to continue his research there. Many eminent scientists pressed him to do so. Hence, he worked there for some time and discovered new things. When an outside stimulus is applied to the muscles of a man or a non-living thing (say a mineral), they respond to it. Bose wondered whether this could happen in a plant also. To test this, he brought a leaf, a carrot and a turnip from the garden. He applied the stimulus. It was confirmed that plants also respond in a similar way. Jagadish Chandra Bose explained this at a meeting of the Royal Society. While explaining his discoveries he said that the Indian sages had understood such principles thousands of years ago. He modestly added that his discoveries were an insignificant part of the great truth that our ancient sages had already realised.

CHAPTER 7
Remarkable Experiments

When anything new is discovered, there will always be people who would question it. The results of Bose's work, too, were not accepted by all. There were people who challenged them and even said that there was not much truth in them. Bose gave a lecture at the Linnean Society to a gathering of scientists. He explained with suitable experiments how plants respond to stimuli. Even those, who had challenged him, could not find fault with his experiments or conclusions.

There is an interesting story about a demonstration that Bose gave in England. On that day, he wanted to show some new things that he had discovered. He had come to the conclusion that plants can feel pain like animals and that when we pinch them they suffer and die in a few minutes, after they are poisoned. Bose wanted to show experiments to prove these conclusions.

A number of scientists and other leading men and women had gathered to hear him. Bose started the experiments by injecting poison into a plant. The plant should have shown signs of death in a few minutes. On the contrary, nothing happened. The learned audience started laughing. Even at this adverse moment, Bose showed admirable calmness. He thought quickly that the poison that he injected into the plant did not kill it. So, he supposed that it would not hurt him as well. With full confidence, he got ready to inject the poison into himself. At that instant, a man got up and confessed that instead of poison he had put similar coloured water. Now, Bose conducted the experiment again with real poison, whereupon, the plant withered and died as expected.

Jagadish Chandra Bose continued his work and made new discoveries. He found that plants shrink a little during the night. He found out why plants always grow towards light, even if they have to bend. He also found out

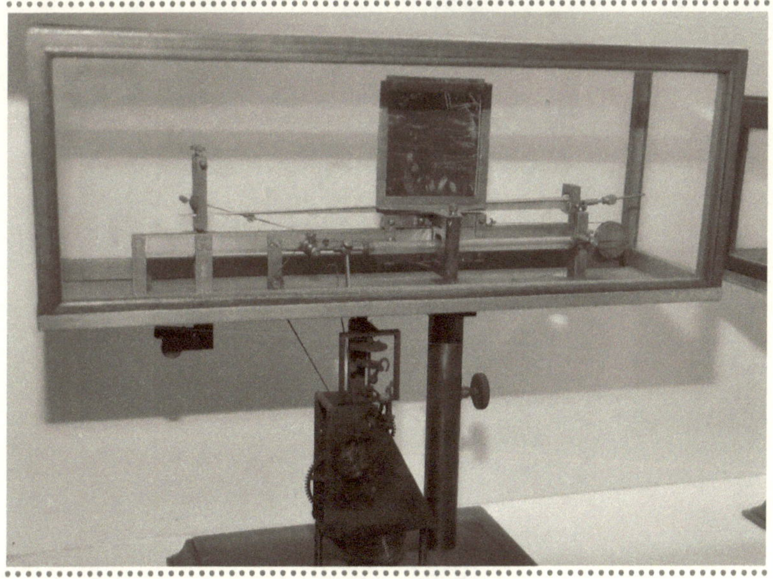

the reason why some plants grow straight while some do not. He explained that this was due to the 'pulsation' in plants. This pulsation quickens by heat and slows down by cold in plants.

Jagadish Chandra Bose did remarkable work and scientists outside India honoured him. Yet, there were people who opposed him. As a result even the Royal Society delayed publishing his valuable work in its publications. But, nothing could make him give up his work. He was sure that years of research had led him to the truth. So, he did not feel that it was very necessary to depend on scientific journals only. He wrote books and published them on his own.

CHAPTER 8
Increased Fame of Bose

By this time, Bose had made a name for himself as a great scientist. The instruments he had developed were being used in some Western countries too. He visited Europe and America in 1907 and 1914, as scientific institutions invited him to explain his discoveries. He visited Japan too.

Most of you have seen a peculiar kind of plant called the mimosa (touch-me-not), which spreads on the ground. It has very small leaves. It is extremely sensitive. If you just touch one leaf, that leaf and the leaves nearby all fold up. The greater the force you use, the larger is the number of leaves that fold up. The whole row of leaves of the branch can be made to fold like this by touching it with a little greater force. Why does only this plant react like this? You have often wondered, haven't you? Bose wondered too. And, he went on to find out. He found that other plants also react to a man's touch in the same way.

The only difference is that you cannot see the reaction of other plants, but you can see the reaction of the mimosa.

But, Bose wanted to study the reaction of other plants too. He designed delicate instruments that would show such reactions in them. When he went abroad, he took these instruments and also some of the plants with him. It was very difficult to keep the plants alive in the climate of foreign countries.

Jagadish Chandra Bose showed the experiment in Cambridge and Oxford. The scientists were fascinated by the extreme sensitivity of plants and they were also filled with wonder when they saw the excellent instruments, which Jagadish Chandra Bose had made himself. No one had done work of this kind in Biology. It was sensational news that plants could also experience different sensations like human beings.

Jagadish Chandra Bose continued his search for new knowledge. His achievements were many. The British Government honoured him more than once. In 1915, when he retired from service, he was made an emeritus professor. He was to get Rs. 1500 per month as long as he lived.

He was honoured as a fellow of the Royal Society (F.R.S) in 1920. In 1927, he presided over the Indian Science Congress.

CHAPTER 9
Establishment of Bose Research Institute

Bose had worked all along without the right kind of scientific instruments and laboratory. For a long time, he had been thinking of building a laboratory. The result was the birth of 'Bose Research Institute', which is located in Calcutta. Even now it is famous as a Centre of Research.

Bose had been collecting funds for this institute for quite some time. More than sixty-five years ago, he had realised the importance of a research institution in India. While inaugurating the Bose Research Institute, he said, "this is not a laboratory but a temple." Such was his devotion to work. He felt everybody must have the same enthusiasm for research in a country. In the Bose Research Institute, research is conducted in Botany and Physics, the two branches of Science in which Bose had won fame.

He worked in this laboratory for 20 years, up to the very end of his life. "We should not depend on others to do our work, we ourselves must do our work, but before we can do this we must get over our pride," was his firm belief. He confessed that he had learnt this lesson from his parents. The Bose Institute, which was to him a temple and not a laboratory, he dedicated to the nation on November 30, 1907. Basu Vigyan Mandir proved a stupendous success in his life. The seer scientist has left an imperishable memorial of himself in his mandir.

J.C. Bose himself started the display of his instruments, which, as a continuous process, made their way into the present museum in the year 1986-87. The main purpose of this technological museum is to display and maintain some of the instruments designed, made and used by Sir J.C. Bose, his personal belongings and memorabilia. The museum is housed in the main campus at 93/ 1 A. P. C. Road and is open on all weekdays. It is a source of attraction for general public, students and scientists. Distinguished scientists, such as Noble laureate Prof. Richard Ernst (Switzerland), Prof. Roger Penrose (U.K.) and Prof. C.J. Gibbins (U.K.) are among the few who visited the museum in the recent past. The activities of the museum are:

- Participation, on request, to display and demonstrate Sir J.C. Bose's equipment in seminars, symposiums and exhibitions organised by both National and International bodies.

- Production of replica of original instruments with the help of Bose institute workshop.

- Offers assistance to National and International bodies in preparing films related to history of Science in India.

- Takes part in manpower training programmes on millimeter wave technology organised by the institute of radiophysics and electronics, Calcutta University and sponsored by Department of Electronics, Govt. of India.

- Acts as a resource point regarding life and works of Sir J.C. Bose to students, scientists, historians and common people.

- Participates in mass awareness programmes in Science through slides and popular lectures.

CHAPTER 10
Activities of Bose Research Institute

These days, it is not surprising to find many research activities today spanning a wide compass, a feature that makes Bose Research Institute unique amongst all research institutes in India. The institute's 600 staff and students mostly work from two campuses in the city of Kolkata, which house its various academic departments and sections, together with a library and other service units. The J.C. Bose museum is a special attraction in the main campus. It houses a fine collection of the manuscripts, instruments, etc. Records of Bose's life and work are on permanent display. In addition, there are four special purpose field stations.

In recent years, the impact of scientific research is assessed on objective criteria, e.g. citation index, impact factors, peer review etc. In an independent assessment of research activities in India by the National Information System for Sciences & Technology (Nissat) of the

Department of Scientific and Industrial Research, the research work from Bose Institute was rated to have high impact in Biology and Biomedical research areas.

The eminence attained by Bose Institute in multi-disciplinary scientific research is evident from the feet that during the last 10 years, 1115 research papers were published in peer reviewed National and International journals and 167 students from the institute were awarded Ph.D. degrees during the period. The high quality of research at the institute attracted more than an extra-mural funding support of more than Rs. 30.00 crores during the last 5 years (9th five year plan). The scientists have received recognition in their respective areas of specialisation from National and International Research Organisations. Current faculty includes two fellows of

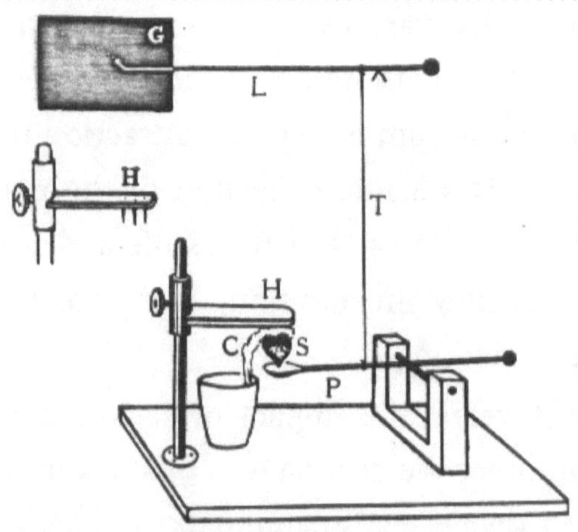

Fig. 20.   Automatic apparatus for recording germination of seeds.

H, seed-holder ; s, seed ; c, wet cotton dipped in water ; P, aluminium pan attached by silk thread T to short arm of recording lever L.

Indian National Science Academy, nine fellows of National Academy of Sciences and six fellows of Indian Academy of Sciences. In addition, several research scientists have been awarded well known fellowships, such as Homi Bhabha fellowship, Nehru fellowship, Rockefeller foundation fellowship, K.S. Krishnan fellowship and young scientists have received the Dst, Dbt and Insa's young scientist awards. The prestigious Darshan Vigyan Samman, the Dbt Young Women Bioscientist Award and Pratima-Sucharu Samman for women scientist of the year 2001 have also been received by Bose Institute scientists. The institute boasts of various departments such as:

- Animal physiology
- Immunotechnology
- Biochemistry
- Microbiology
- Biophysics
- Physics
- Botany
- P.M. C.G.
- Chemistry
- Workshop
- Environment

CHAPTER 11
The Scientific Thinker

Nature had always been a source of attraction right from his early age, to Bose. The flowers on plants, flowers giving fruits, the leaves falling off, seeds germinating into new plants, attracted Bose the most.

He was interested in these happenings, which to many people seem quite ordinary. He asked questions to others as well as himself, "how do these things happen?" But, not always could he satisfy his curiosity. It was his way to try to find answers to questions arising in his mind that brought him the world fame.

You may consider here the more important of his discoveries. Plants respond to stimulus from outside. You draw away hand when it touches fire. When it is extremely cold you may even die. Plants also experience heat and cold in this way. This can be measured with a thermometer. At 60 degrees centigrade, a plant will faint because of the extreme heat and, at very low temperatures, it will react similarly to cold. Plants always react to the rise or fall in temperature in the atmosphere around them.

When heat or cold is extreme, plants will faint or may even die. Bose had designed very delicate instruments that could record this change. When a plant is hurt at one point, the shock of this is transmitted to all the other parts and the whole plant gets tired and it bends down. Plants grow every second by 1/50,000th of an inch! How is this to be measured - it is extremely small? Bose himself devised a delicate instrument, which could measure even that length.

Plants do not grow in a perfect straight line. There are small twists and turns, why? The answer that Bose found out is very interesting. He said that plants have positive and negative charges. If one of these pushes a part of the plant forward, the other pushes it backward. The growth of the plant is affected by these pushes and it becomes slightly curved instead of being straight. Plants grow towards light even when kept in a dark place, why? The roots of plants always grow downwards, why? Bose found answers to all these questions.

CHAPTER 12
Demonstration by Bose

You all know that the lovely flower, the lotus, opens up as the sun rises in the sky. When the sun sets, the lotus closes its petals. The popular belief is that this is because the lotus loves the sun. But, Bose explained this peculiar behaviour of the lotus. It opens when there is a rise in the temperature and closes, as the temperature drops. Same happens in the case of sunflower. He called this peculiarity –'the thirst for light'. The other peculiar thing he demonstrated was the way plants behave differently at different times of the day. He established that from 6 in the morning to 3 o'clock in the afternoon, the plants behave in one way and from 3 in the afternoon to 6 in the morning, plants behave differently. As an example, he chose a palm tree in Faridpur.

This palm in Faridpur would bend down every evening. The people of the place had their own explanation. They believed that the soul of some holy man lived in the tree. They believed that every evening, when the temple bells rang, this holy spirit bowed in devotion. But Jagadish

Chandra Bose discovered the real cause. He gave a scientific explanation. The tree bent down in the evening and raised itself in the morning because of the fall and the rise in the temperature.

Water is very essential to plants. The roots of the plants absorb water. But even without roots too, plants can absorb water. This was demonstrated by Bose. He showed that when the root is cut and the plant stem is placed in water, it starts absorbing water. Suppose you remove the plant from the soil and place it upside down (with the branches below and the roots above), what happens? The leaves and the stem absorb water. Bose proved this by the means of experiments.

The cells of a plant function like a man's heart, the heart contracts and expands to pump blood, and in the same way, the cells of a plant expand and contract.

This had to be proved by experiments. So, Bose himself devised a new instrument, which could show how the cells worked.

CHAPTER 13
Bose and Tagore

Jagadish Chandra Bose was famous as a scientist. He brought laurels to his motherland. But, his interests were many-sided. He was also interested in literature and

fine arts. The great poet Rabindranath Tagore and Jagadish Chandra Bose were very good friends. The first time, when Tagore visited Bose, he was not at home. Tagore left a bunch of champak flowers for him. This was the beginning of their friendship.

Tagore invited Bose to stay with him for some time. Bose agreed to do so, on one condition. The condition was that Tagore should narrate a story to him every day. This is how a number of Tagore's stories came to be written. Have you read the story *The Kabuliwallah*? It is a very fine story, as it narrates how a deep and strange friendship grew up between a rough Pathan and a little Bengali girl. This has been translated into several languages and is well known in a number of countries. Tagore wrote this story when Bose was staying with him.

Verily, Jagadish Chandra's *avyakta* (the unmanifest) is one of the few to be chewed and digested. Here, the style, the analysis and arguments are vigorous. Reading between the lines of this unique work of his, we can easily form the idea that he was an expositor of rare rounded knowledge. While presenting the book to his life-long bosom friend, Rabindranath, he wrote,

"Friend,

Around you are entwined the memories of years of my joy and sorrow. Today I send into the glare of your sunlight the glimmer of my glow-worm.

Yours,

Jagadish"

Rabindranath's immediate reply too was arresting and it threw much light on Jagadish Chandra's literary genius. He wrote,

"Friend,

Much of your *avyakta* is well known to me... although you have science as your first love, yet well could literature claim that coveted place. It is only by your inattention that she stands neglected.

Yours,

Rabi"

And Bose, the great scientist, was also the president of the Bengali Sahitya Parishad.

You have already seen how Bose honoured the Indian sages of the past. Scientists of other countries praised Bose's important discoveries. Bose used to say "the sages of India knew all this long ago".

CHAPTER 14
On Personal Front

Bose loved to visit the various shrines of India. Accompanied by his wife, he would make these trips whenever he could find time. He used to take photographs of the places he visited and had quite a collection of these photographs. He went to places of historical or mythological interest. The famous sculptures and the temple architecture of Indian land always thrilled him.

To The Scholars

I leave you my best wishes. I want you to grow into true manhood, strong and self-reliant. Follow only the one object you have chosen. Cast off all small things, meanness and jealousy. Try to be proud of each other's success. Do not talk much but do things. I have tried my utmost for you under many difficulties. Justify my ...

J.C. Bose

He visited Sanchi, Chittorgarh, Ajmer and Nainital, as well as the Cave Temples of Orissa and the famous Ajanta and Ellora Caves. He visited the Puri Jagannatha Swamy Temple. He also visited well-known places of pilgrimage of South India, like Rameshwaram, Madurai and Tanjore. He visited the shrines at the foot of Himalayas. Kedarnath particularly appealed to him.

Jagadish Chandra Bose was not a proud man. He was simple, affectionate and warm. It is not surprising that many great persons of the day were his friends. Prafulla Chandra Ray, another famous scientist, was one of his close friends. Eminent men, like Gopalakrishna Gokhale and Mahatma Gandhi, knew and respected him. Sister Nivedita was another good friend. She was an Irish lady. Her name was Margaret Nobel. She was the disciple of Swami Vivekananda. She settled down in India and spent her life in the service of the people of this country. She recognised the genius in Bose. Bose toiled hard to educate the people about the importance of Science and Sister Nivedita admired his efforts. So, she was keenly looking forward to the birth of the Bose Research Institute. In memory of her, Bose placed in front of the institute the statue of a woman stepping forward with a light in her hand.

He had another good friend, Mrs. Bull. While touring America, he was her guest. She had taken care of him like a mother. When he fell ill in Paris, she travelled to Paris, made arrangements for his treatment and personally looked after him. There were his two other friends, two giants of the literary world. They were George Bernard Shaw, the English dramatist and Romain Rolland, the French writer. Both of them dedicated one book each to Jagadish Chandra Bose.

CHAPTER 15
Abala Bose

It is imperatively necessary to write a few words about Bose's wife, Lady Abala Bose. She was a personality of tremendous executive drive and precision. She was, at once, his guide and disciple as necessity demanded. Sister Nivedita and many other eminent figures remained beholden to this venerable woman till the end of their lives.

Jagadish Chandra Bose was very busy throughout his life. He had no time to think of the problems of the household. His wife, Abala Bose, looked after their home all by herself. She was herself a student of medicine, when her marriage to Bose was settled. Bose's parents were very kind and generous, as they had helped many people with money. At the time of Bose's marriage, the family was in heavy debts. Jagadish Chandra Bose had to repay the debts. So, Abala Bose was extremely careful in spending money and saved as much as possible. Unfortunately, the Bose couple had only one child, who did not live long. They looked after the students as their children. Abala Bose started girls' school in Calcutta and took upon herself the responsibility of maintaining it. She went with her husband when he went to foreign countries and even helped in his scientific work.

Jagadish Chandra Bose has a permanent place in the world of Science, especially in Botany. He began the age of modern Science in India and deserves honour for this. He had all the qualities that research requires. He had keen powers of observation and was patient. He was also a very good lecturer. His students loved his lectures. He did not teach only for the sake of the examination. Students should study books and study what the teacher teaches, but this is not enough, they should use their brains and think for themselves, they should be eager to discover new knowledge - this is what he taught his students. He encouraged them to observe, to experiment and to think, without depending only on books and teachers.

Jagadish Chandra Bose died in November 1937. To the very end, he was busy with research.

Wealth and power never attracted Jagadish Chandra Bose. He toiled for science selflessly like a saint. This great scientist is a great example to all.

CHAPTER 16
An Experiment on Electromagnetic Waves

In 1895, Bose gave his first public demonstration of electromagnetic waves, using them to ring a bell remotely and to explode some gunpowder. In 1896, the daily chronicle of England reported, "the inventor (J.C. Bose) has transmitted signals to a distance of nearly a mile and herein lies the first and obvious and exceedingly valuable application of this new theoretical marvel."

Popov in Russia was doing similar experiments, but had written in December 1895 that he was still entertaining the hope of remote signaling with radio waves. The first successful wireless signaling experiment by Marconi on Salisbury-plain, in England, was not to happen until May 1897. The 1895 public demonstration by Bose, in Calcutta, predates all these experiments. Invited by Lord Rayleigh, in 1897, Bose reported on his microwave (millimeter wave) experiments to the Royal Institution and other societies in England. The wavelengths he used ranged from 2.5 cm to 5 mm. In his presentation to the Royal Institution, in January 1897, Bose speculated on the existence of electromagnetic radiation from the sun, suggesting that either the solar or the terrestrial atmosphere might be responsible for the lack of success so far in detecting such radiation. Solar emission was not detected until 1942 and the 1.2 cm atmospheric water vapour absorption line was discovered during experimental radar work in 1944. By about the end of the 19th century, the interests of Bose turned away from electromagnetic waves to response phenomena in plants. This included studies of the effects of electromagnetic radiation on plants, a topical field today.

On May 10, 1901, the hall of the Royal Society in London was packed with eminent scientists. They were watching Jagadish Chandra Bose conduct experiments to show that plants and metals have feelings. The plant, with its roots, was carefully picked up and dipped up to its stem in a vessel containing bromide, a poison. Bose looked expectantly at the light spot on a screen meant to indicate the pulse of the plant. So did everyone else.

The plant's pulse beat, which the spot recorded as a steady to-and-fro movement like the pendulum of a clock, began to grow unsteady. Soon, the spot vibrated violently and then came to a sudden stop. It was almost like a poisoned rat breathing heavily and jerking its legs and tail in its struggle against death. The plant had died because of the poison.

CHAPTER 17
Achievements of Bose

The experiment on plant was greeted with thunderous applause. However, some physiologists, who were studying the processes that took place inside a living organism, were not happy. Not only was Bose, a physicist, an intruder into their field, but he had, by his experiments, upset the well-known theories of some eminent physiologists present there. They were critical of Bose's conclusion that 'plants and metals have life'. They urged the Royal Society not to publish his lecture unless he made certain changes. Bose refused to make these changes and his experiments went unnoticed for a while. He was, however, not a person to accept defeat easily. He had acquired the quality to fight against odds from his childhood.

To professor Bose, scientific research was nothing other than the life principle itself. As the spiritual thirst in him was great, he grew bold to say in a wonderful speech delivered at the Royal Institute, London, that, "they who behold the one, in all the changing manifoldness of the universe, unto them belongs the eternal truth, unto none else, unto none else."

It was on his 36th birthday that Bose decided to devote himself to pure research. Oliver Lodge's paper on Heinrich Hertz and his successors had inspired him so much that he began to conduct research on what is today known as 'radio waves'. Although he did not get any facility or money from the college, he made the equipment he needed within three months and embarked upon his research. The training in metal turning and carpentry that he had received in his teens came in handy. Later, this very training enabled him to fabricate many sensitive instruments for plant studies.

Although Bose is more famous as a biologist, he was a great physicist as well. He can rightly be called the

inventor of wireless telegraphy. In 1895, a year before Guglielmo Marconi patented this invention, he had demonstrated its functioning in public. He was the first to fabricate the device that generated microwaves and radio waves of very short wavelength. Also, he was the first to use these microwaves to understand the structure of materials. One of the devices he had fabricated, now called the 'waveguide', forms an essential component of several sophisticated electronic and nuclear equipments.

CHAPTER 18
Stepping Ladders of Success

Bose also fabricated a highly sensitive 'coherer', the device that detects radio waves. In fact, it was due to his detailed research that he switched from Physics to the study of metals and then plants. He found that the sensitivity of the coherer decreased when it was used continuously for a long period. In other words, it became tired. And, indeed, when he gave the device some rest, it regained its sensitivity, which clearly indicated that metals have feelings and memory. The metals that are used daily, such as a knife, are not dead but unconscious, like a badly beaten man. They enter this state when they are heated and molded.

Bose also invented several sensitive instruments. The most wonderful was the Cresco graph, an instrument to measure the rate of growth of a plant. How sensitive this instrument was, can be imagined from the fact that it could measure plant growth that was 20,000 times less than a snail's speed.

Bose arrived at the conclusion that plants and metals have life on the basis of the electric nature of living things. When a part of the body feels pain, nerves carry electric signals from it to the brain for information. Similarly, when a hand is to be moved, the brain communicates the order to do so by an electric signal. So, also the brain, muscles and heart in an animal function on electric signals. Bose showed experimentally that, though plants do not have a brain, muscle or heart, there are small cells in them, which behave in the same manner. The only difference between the response of a plant and of an animal is that of time. A plant takes a longer time to respond.

Although Bose did most of his experiments in Calcutta, not many of his countrymen recognised their importance. Notable exceptions were Mahatma Gandhi, Rabindranath Tagore and Swami Vivekananda.

Bose made waves in Calcutta as Hertz had done in Karlsruhe. He produced some thirteen papers: 7 in the proceedings of the Royal Society, one in Philosophical Magazine and the others in the Electrician.

The ordeal of scientific solitude was temporarily broken in 1896, when Bose made the voyage to England. At the meeting of the British Association of Advancement of Science, Liverpool, he demonstrated his apparatus for the study of the properties of electric waves. History was being made, his wife recorded, as Bose stood in front of the world, prepared to wage the battle in the realm of Science. Among those present, she saw Oliver Lodge, Lord

Kelvin and J.J. Thomson. The ageing Kelvin limped up to the gallery and congratulated her on her husband's work.

On Friday, January 29,1897, Bose delivered at the Royal Institution the famed 'evening discourse' on 'the electromagnetic radiation and the polarisation of the electric ray'. The University of London conferred on him the D.Sc. Degree for his work on electric waves. Bose's discourse gave a clear indication that his was the work of one belonging to a cultural tradition, which was not rooted in Europe. It was also, as much, the realisation of Sir Car's vision of scientific research in India.

CHAPTER 19
Comments of Eminent Personalities

Vivekananda

In 1900, an international exhibition of scientific research was held in Paris. Many eminent scientists, from all parts of the world, gathered there to offer their contributions. The spiritual giant Swami Vivekananda happened to attend it. Highly impressed by the admirable achievements of Bose, his heart pined to see a son of Bengal who could walk shoulder to shoulder with mighty figures. Suddenly, to his astonishment, the magnetic personality of J.C. Bose caught his attention. He was overjoyed to find his Bengali brother eclipsing his colleagues. His assertion about Bose was, "today Jagadish Bose—an Indian, a loving son of Bengal-heads the list of the galaxy of scientists. Three times three cheers for Jagadish Chandra!"

A report that appeared in a London daily stated, if you watch his astonishing experiments with plants and flowers, you have to leave an old world behind and enter a new one. The world where plants are merely plants becomes mercilessly out of date and you are forced abruptly into a world where plants are almost human beings. Professor Bose makes you take the leap when he demonstrates that plants have a nervous system quite comparable with that of men and makes them write down their life-story.

Sri Aurobindo

The seer scientist revealed to the world that metal, too, possesses signs of life. To quote Sri Aurobindo, the master of integral yoga, "a bridge has been built between man and inert matter. If we take Dr. Bose's experiments with metals in conjunction with his experiments on plants, we may hold it to be practically proved for the thinker that life in various degrees of manifestation and organisation is omnipresent in matter and is no foreign introduction or accidental development, but was always there to be evolved. Mind, which modern Science has not yet begun to rightly investigate, awaits its turn."

Bose gave a revealing intimation of the truth that man must seek brotherhood today, so that he may grow capable of liberating himself from the clutches of the feeling of superiority that threatens to eclipse the sun of true civilisation.

Comments from the scientists of Vienna

"You have left us nothing to do!", such was the glowing tribute paid to Bose by the scientists of Vienna after observing his investigations, so complete and perfect.

Their sincere appreciation of Bose fairly indicates that he stood head and shoulders above his contemporaries in the world of Science.

George Bernard Shaw

While presenting his works to Bose, George Bernard Shaw, who is known all over the world for his challenging plays, for his love of fun, his keen wit and his sharp criticism, wrote,

"From the lowest physiologist to the greatest physiologist of the world."

CHAPTER 20
Bose: An Inference of Life

The seer scientist successfully crossed the barrier between physics and physiology. He also crossed the barrier between the living and the non-living just to inform the world of his rare realisation that there is but one truth, which simultaneously embraces all branches of knowledge. He admitted the fact that public life and various other professions will be the appropriate spheres of activity for aspiring young men. But, he desired something more from the those few, "I call those very few who, after realising an inner call, will devote their whole life with strengthened character and determined purpose to participate in the infinite struggle to win knowledge for its own sake and see truth face to face."

Sri Jagadish Chandra Bose is an immortal name in the scientific world. It wouldn't be wrong to call him a born scientist. He was the forerunner of a new age of scientific research. He had moved the frontiers of intuitive Science towards a fresh attainment. A man of deep faith, a perfect example of artless living and lofty thinking, an embodiment of all that is good and inspiring was Jagadish Chandra.

'Sarvam Prana Ejati Nihsrtam' (Everything springs up from life and makes movements therein).

This eternal message of the Upanishads ceaselessly reverberated in the innermost recesses of the discoverer of plant sensitivity'. The world has come to learn from this son of India, the secret of observing a plant shivering, suffering, struggling, perhaps even reciprocating love. For him, the modern world would have remained quite in the dark about the deeds and misdeeds of the plants so near and dear to the mother earth and us as well. His approach to the scientific world was absolutely original. Although his apparatus did not demand of him a heavy charge, yet, strangely enough, by virtue of his skill, he won the greatest honour.

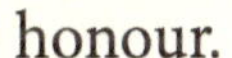

"Science and art belong to the whole world and before them vanish the barriers of nationality."— Goethe.

The Indian scientist sees eye to eye with the mighty poet. He even takes one step further,

"Nothing is as far from truth as saying that

the world is indebted to some particular nation for its progress in the sphere of knowledge. All countries of the world are interdependent. This attitude of interdependence forges the bond of unity and determines the pause and progress of civilisation."

CHAPTER 21
The Creator of Wireless Communications

Nearly 100 years after Guglielmo Marconi's first transatlantic wireless communication, it has come to light that the detector he had used to pick up the signal was invented by Professor Jagadish Chandra Bose. The discovery made by a group of scientists of a US-based Institute proves what has been a century-old suspicion in the World Scientific Community: that the honour of being the pioneer in wireless communication should have gone to Bose and not Marconi.

Bose's invention of the mercury coherer with a telephone, which Marconi used, was published in the proceedings of the Royal Society, London, on April 27, 1899, over two years before Marconi's first wireless communication on December 12, 1901, from Newfoundland, now in Canada. In January 1998, the IEEE published a special issue, where evidence was presented to show that Marconi had used the sensitive semiconductor diode device invented by Bose.

Investigations by the IEEE group show that both Bose and Marconi were in London in 1896-97. The Italian scientist was conducting wireless experiments for the British post office and Bose was on a lecture tour. Both scientists were interviewed by McClure's magazine (now defunct) in March 1897. In the interview, Bose came out with high praise for Marconi, who was then under attack from established British scientists who doubted his credentials. Marconi never could make it to college because of his poor high school record. Bose also said that he was not interested in commercial telegraphy and that others could use his research work.

In 1899, Bose unveiled his invention of the mercury coherer with the telephone detector on a paper at the Royal Society. In a curious coincidence, Bose lost his diary containing an account of the invention and a prototype of the detector during a lecture tour in the same year. Brilliant Marconi quickly grasped the commercial importance of Bose's invention and began to explore it secretly. His childhood friend Luigi Solan started experimenting with Bose's invention and presented Marconi with a slightly modified design in the summer of 1901 for use in the upcoming transatlantic experiment.

The Italian scientist then went on to apply for a British patent in his name, never acknowledging his debt to Bose. Securing Bose's place in the history of long-distance communication, the IEEE paper narrates how the truth was suppressed all these years, even though it was there for all to see in the 1899 proceedings of the Royal Society. A combination of factors like innocence about patenting, plain misfortune and politics of the contemporary times weighed against Bose.

Just one hundred years ago, J.C. Bose described to the Royal Institution in London his research carried out in Calcutta at millimeter wavelengths. He used waveguides, horn antennas, dielectric lenses, various polarisers and even semiconductors at frequencies as high as 60 GHz, much of his original equipments are still in existence, now at the Bose Institute in Calcutta. Some concepts from his original 1897 papers have been incorporated into a new 1.3 mm multi-beam receiver now in use on the 12 metre telescope.

CHAPTER 22
Researches of Bose

James Clerk Maxwell's equations predicting the existence of electromagnetic radiation propagating at the speed of light were made public in 1865. In 1888, Hertz had demonstrated generation of electromagnetic waves and that their properties were similar to those of light. Before the start of the twentieth century, many of the concepts now familiar in microwaves, had been developed. The list includes the cylindrical parabolic reflector, dielectric lens, microwave absorbers, the cavity radiator, the radiating iris and the pyramidal electromagnetic horn. Round, square and rectangular waveguides were used, with experimental development anticipating Rayleigh's 1896 theoretical solution by several years for wave-guide modes.

Hertz had used a wavelength of 66 cm. Other 'post-Hertzian pre-1900' experimenters used wavelengths well into the short cm-wave region, with Bose in Calcutta and Lebedew in Moscow independently performing experiments at wavelengths as short as 5 and 6 mm.

One of Bose's lecturers at Cambridge was Professor Rayleigh, who clearly had a profound influence on his later work. In 1884, Bose was awarded a B.A. from Cambridge and also a B.Sc. from London University. Bose then returned to India, taking up a post, initially, as officiating professor of physics at the Presidency College in Calcutta. Following the example of Lord Rayleigh, Jagadish Chandra Bose made extensive use of scientific demonstrations in class. He is reported as being extraordinarily popular and effective as a teacher. Many of his students at the Presidency College were destined to become famous in their own right, for example S.N. Bose, later became well-known for the Bose-Einstein statistics.

A book by Sir Oliver Lodge, 'Heinrich Hertz and his successors', impressed Bose. In 1894, J.C. Bose converted a small enclosure adjoining a bathroom in the Presidency College into a laboratory. He carried out experiments involving refraction, diffraction and polarisation. To receive the radiation, he used a variety of different junctions connected to a highly sensitive galvanometer. He plotted in detail the voltage-current characteristics of his junctions, noting their non-linear characteristics. He developed the use of galena crystals for making receivers, both for short wavelength radio waves and for white and ultraviolet light. Patent rights for their use in detecting electromagnetic radiation were granted to him in 1904. In 1954, Pearson and Brattain gave priority to Bose for the use of a semi-conducting crystal as a detector of radio waves.

CHAPTER 23
Apparatus of Bose

Sir Neville Mott, Nobel laureate in 1977 for his own contributions to solid-state electronics, remarked that "J.C. Bose was at least 60 years ahead of his time" and "in fact, he had anticipated the existence of p-type and n-type semiconductors."

He retired from the Presidency College in 1915, but was appointed as an emeritus professor. Two years later, the Bose Institute was founded. Bose was elected as a fellow of the Royal Society in 1920.

He died in 1937, a week before his 80th birthday, his ashes are in a shrine at the Bose institute in Calcutta.

Bose's experiments were carried out at the Presidency College in Calcutta, although for demonstrations, he developed a compact portable version of the equipment, including transmitter, receiver and various microwave components. Some of his original equipment still exists, now at the Bose Institute in Calcutta.

Bose measured the characteristics of his junctions, an example characteristic curve of a 'single point iron receiver'. The junction consisted of a sharp point of iron, pressing against an iron surface, with pressure capable of fine adjustment. The different curves correspond to different contact pressures. Bose noted that the junction does not obey Ohm's law and that there is a knee in the curve at approximately 0.45 volts, the junction becomes most effective at detection of short wavelength radiation when the corresponding bias voltage is applied. He made further measurements on a variety of junctions made of different materials, classifying the different materials into positive or negative classes of substance. In one experiment, he noted that increasing the applied voltage to the junction actually decreased the resulting current, implying a negative dynamic resistance. Bose experimented with samples of jute in polarising experiments. In one experiment, he made a twisted bundle of jute and showed that it could be used to rotate the plane of polarisation. The modern equivalent component may be a twisted dielectric waveguide. He further used this to construct a macroscopic molecular model as an analogy to the rotation of polarisation produced by liquids like sugar solutions.

One investigation involved measurement of total internal reflection inside a dielectric prism and the effect of a small air gap between two identical prisms. When the prisms are widely separated, total internal reflection takes place and the incident radiation is reflected inside the dielectric. When the 2 prisms touch, radiation propagates unhindered through both prisms. By introducing a small air gap, the combination becomes a variable attenuator to incident radiation.

CHAPTER 24
Contribution of Bose

Bose made an investigation of this prism attenuator experimentally. The results of the experiment were published in the events of the Royal Society in November 1897. In 1910 Schaefer and Gross studied the prism combination theoretically and the device has since being described in standard texts.

At the National Radio Astronomy Observator in Tucson, Arizona, a new multiple-feed receive working at a wavelength of 1.3 mm, has been built lately. It has been installed on the 12 metre telescope at kitt peak. The system is an 8-feet receiver. The local oscillator is being injected optically into the superconducting tunnel junction (sis) mixers. The power level of the injected local oscillator with a mixer receiver is critical. Here, each of the 8 mixers needs to have independent local oscillator power adjustment.

Conclusions:

J.C. Bose had undertaken the research into the generation and detection of millimetre waves and the properties of substances at these wavelengths in some details. This research was undertaken by him one hundred years ago in Calcutta.

Most of the microwave components known today, for example waveguide, horn antennas, polarisers, dielectric lenses, prisms and even semiconductor detectors of electromagnetic radiation, were invented and utilised in last decade of the nineteenth century. Towards the end of the century, many people working in this area developed their interests in other topics.

Attention of the wireless experimenters of the time became focused on much longer wavelengths which, eventually, with the help of the then unknown ionosphere, were able to support signaling at very much greater distances.

Though it seems that Bose's demonstration of remote wireless signaling has precedence over Marconi, he was the first who used a semiconductor junction for detecting radio waves and he made inventions, like various now commonplace microwave components. Outside India, he was not often given the deserved recognition. Later his further work at millimeter wavelengths was almost non-existent for almost 50 years. So, it can be said that J.C. Bose was, at least, much ahead of his time. He will always be remembered for his notable contribution in this field.